Fiona's Story
Featuring Fiona the Sea Turtle

Dedicated to all those who work so diligently to rescue and provide shelter and medical treatment for sea turtles

Presented by Rescue Pups and Such
Book series inspired by real-life rescue animals

Written and Illustrated by Connie Wenzel
Edited by Cortney Warsh
Graphic Design by Dial Graphics, WPB, Florida
*Second Edition

Fiona the sea turtle lived in the ocean.

Fiona loved to swim around and look at all the beautiful and vibrant colors on the ocean floor.

One day Fiona was accidentally caught in a fishing net.

With all of her might she tried to free herself from the net, but the more she struggled the more tangled she became.

After awhile, she felt sad and defeated so she stopped struggling.

Fiona thought she would never swim happy and free again.

Exhausted and unable to swim,
Fiona floated to the ocean surface.

Suddenly, a strong wave
washed Fiona onto a beach.

Night fell and the moon was shining bright.
Still trapped in the net,
Fiona was too tired to move.

Fiona lost all hope of freeing herself.

As the sun rose, Fiona's eyes became too heavy to keep open.

She fell fast asleep and dreamed she was happy and free swimming in the ocean.

Later that morning a boy walking on the beach noticed something in the sand. It was Fiona trapped in the net!

The boy leaned over Fiona and said, "Don't worry, I'm going to call for help!"

Minutes later, an ambulance from the turtle rescue drove onto the beach and found Fiona!

A man jumped out of the ambulance and freed her from the net.

Fiona was so happy to be free and couldn't wait to go back into the ocean!

Instead, she was placed on a stretcher and carried to the ambulance.

Fiona was so confused.
Why wasn't she going back into the ocean?

"Oh no!" Fiona thought.
"Will I ever see the ocean again?"

After a short drive, the ambulance arrived at the turtle rescue.

A doctor examined Fiona at the rescue. "You have some injuries," he said. "I'll give you some medicine and soon you'll feel good as new."

Fiona then understood why the man from the ambulance didn't return her to the ocean... she needed to get better first!

Fiona started to have hope again!
Hope that one day
she would return home!

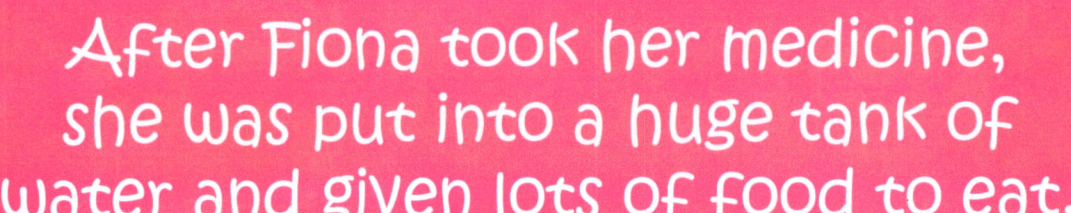

After Fiona took her medicine, she was put into a huge tank of water and given lots of food to eat.

Fiona felt much better in the water. She became very hungry and ate all of her food.

Every morning Fiona was
so excited to see Faith
and spend the day with her.

Fiona was happy at the turtle rescue
but missed spending her days
swimming in the ocean.

One morning Faith ran to Fiona with tears in her eyes and said, "I have news!"

Fiona wondered, "What's wrong with Faith?
Why is she crying?
Will I never be well enough to go home?"

"You're all better!" Faith said.
"You're going home to the ocean!"

Faith was crying because she was so happy for Fiona!

Fiona thought, "Is it true? Am I really going back to the ocean? Will I be swimming free again?"

Fiona was so happy that she also started to cry!

The next day the ambulance brought Fiona back to the same beach where she was found.

Fiona's release was big news! People from all over the country came to watch her return to the ocean.

Fiona was carefully placed onto the sand.
She looked back and saw Faith smiling at her.

Fiona and Faith both knew their season of friendship had come to an end.
With a sad heart, Fiona started to pull herself towards the water.

Fiona then heard everyone clapping and cheering for her. The louder they cheered the more excited Fiona became. She pulled herself faster and faster towards the water until a wave splashed her face!

Fiona could still hear the crowd cheering as she swam away from the beach.

Fiona kept swimming out farther and farther until she could no longer see the beach.

Fiona was so happy to be free!
Free to swim! Free to once again see all the beautiful and vibrant colors in the ocean.

www.ingramcontent.com/pod-product-compliance
Lightning Source LLC
Chambersburg PA
CBHW042145290426
44110CB00002B/124